Do G😎D Stuff ™

NEW YORK

The Official Do Good Stuff™ Journal

Published in New York, New York, by Morgan James Publishing. Morgan James and The Entrepreneurial Publisher are trademarks of Morgan James, LLC.

Morgan James Publishing, The Entrepreneurial Publisher
5 Penn Plaza, 23rd Floor, New York City, New York 10001
(212) 655-5470 office • (516) 908-4496 fax
www.MorganJamesPublishing.com

This is a trustworthy saying, and I want you to insist on these teachings so that all who trust in God will devote themselves to doing good. These teachings are good and beneficial for everyone. - Titus 3:8 NLT

9781630479282   paperback
9781630479299   hardcover

Library of Congress Control Number: 2015921108

Cover Design Trademarked by:
Joel Comm

Produced by:
Brittany Bondar

In an effort to support local communities, raise awareness and funds, Morgan James Publishing donates a percentage of all book sales for the life of each book to Habitat for Humanity Peninsula and Greater Williamsburg.

Get involved today, visit
www.MorganJamesBuilds.com

www.DoGoodStuff.com

Printed in the USA
CPSIA information can be obtained
at www.ICGtesting.com
JSHW021956150824
68134JS00055B/1911

9 781630 479282